German Dolls
Character Children
& Babies
Volume II

By Patricia R. Smith

COLLECTOR BOOKS
P.O. Box 3009
Paducah, KY 42001

The current values in this book should be used only as a guide. They are not intended to set prices, which vary from one section of the country to another. Auction prices as well as dealer prices vary greatly and are affected by condition as well as demand. Neither the Author nor the Publisher assumes responsibility for any losses that might be incurred as a result of consulting this guide.

Cover Doll: Simon & Halbig's "Erika". Courtesy Irene Brown.

Additional copies of this book may be ordered from:

COLLECTOR BOOKS
P.O. Box 3009
Paducah, Kentucky 42001

@ $9.95 Add $1.00 for postage and handling.

Copyright: Patricia R. Smith, 1980
ISBN: 0-89145-151-X

Printed by IMAGE GRAPHICS, Paducah, Kentucky

We wish to thank the following for sharing the fun of making this Volume II come alive. It was fun working with the dolls, posing them and enjoying the companionship the dolls bring about.

All photos by Dwight Smith unless noted.

Lilah Beck, photos by Renie Culp.
Barbara Boury, photos by Robert Turchan
Elaine Boyle, photos by Elaine Boyle
Irene Brown
Elizabeth Burke, photos by Gunner Burke
Renie Culp, photos by Renie Culp
Shirley Derr
Barbara Earnshaw
Martha Gragg
O.D. Gregg, photos by O.D. Gregg
Diane Hoffman
Olive Krol, photos by Rita Johnson
Roberta Lago, photos by Ted Long
Pat Landis, photos by Pat Landis
Margaret Mandel, photos by Margaret Mandel
Penny Pendlebury, photos by Chuck
Betty Shelly
Mary Sweeney, photos by Mary Sweeney
Cathy Turchan, photos by Robert Turchan
Josephine Wingfield
Gloyra Woods, photos by Gloyra Woods

CONTENTS

DOLLS MADE IN GERMANY

To compete with the quality French doll makers, the German devised methods of mass production which resulted in cheaper dolls that were, basically, copies of the style of doll being sold very successfully by the French. By 1900 just about half of all dolls produced in the world came from Germany. The two largest areas of production were in Bavaria and Thuringia.

In Thuringia, the main center for dolls, everything necessary to make reasonably priced dolls was present, such as skilled workers whose families had been making dolls for several generations, abundance of fire clay and wood was handy for the use in heating some kilns and for making doll limbs although by 1900 coal was commonly used. The German Government provided assistance and revenue to the doll making industry and even assistance to set up schools teaching the design and making of dolls.

Germany's early attempts at copying the French Bebe's, produced kid (leather) bodied dolls which were slimmer and almost straight, without a tucked in waist line. These bodies were cheaper to produce and when dressed the bodies didn't show. Although shoulder head/kid body dolls were made well into the 1920's, they are generally considered to be early types of girl dolls made in Germany. A great many – actually a majority of these early, cheaper dolls from Germany were sold in a chemise, and it is rare to find an originally outfitted doll where the clothes can be attributed to the manufacturer. Most of the early clothes found on a German doll were home stitched, but well made costumes.

Germany kid (leather) bodied dolls often have black fabric used for the lower legs to represent stockings and was another shortcut in cost. Dolls with a slightly better quality had composition lower arms and legs and the best were given bisque lower arms.

Because of the Tariff laws that went into effect in 1890

that made it necessary for all items to be marked with the country of origin, it makes dating some dolls much easier. It must also be noted that dolls made in other countries, to be sold in their own countries, were not required to have more than a mold number, or makers name or both. These "unmarked" dolls often found their way into the U.S. by collectors shopping abroad, or the dolls being sent to the U.S. for sale, or as gifts. As with everything regarding our hobby, careful note should be given this fact.

Many of the German doll makers were very business orientated, such as Armand Marseille and J.D. Kestner, or Kammer and Reinhardt. It makes research of date and patents easier, plus we have earlier doll researchers such as Gwen White, Louella Hart and the Coleman Family to thank for compiling a great many dates and patents together into one book, which makes our task of identification much easier.

No matter what we do, where we look and what we know, some dolls are completely unidentifiable. We can suspect that one of these unmarked dolls may fit a particular maker's style, but unless we have seen the exact mold fully marked, we can only be guessing. Many unmarked molds will have a number, such as 6, 12 or 14 and this usually will denote the mold size of the head.

Most collectors are aware of the copies made of popular modern dolls . . . such as Shirley Temple, Barbies and others, and it must be concluded that this practice has always been a part of the doll making business. We have been able to achieve knowledge on the basic German makers who were famous, and whose dolls can be found in quantity, but there were hundreds of small German companies producing dolls also.

The early Twentieth Century brought about the opinion for a greater understanding of a child's basic needs and a great upsurge of interest in the psychology of the child. During this period makers began to commission artists to create dolls that would satisfy the child, and before long nearly all the major German doll factories considered making character dolls as part of their line. Although most continued to make the stylized, "dolly" faced dolls they had produced for years, a great many companies followed through with making some character dolls.

The earliest "character" baby heads were made on unusual kid (leather) bodies that looked as if they had just been cut down versions of the normal child type body. The bent limb composition baby body was first advertised in 1904 and was an immediate success. Assembly was fast as there were only five parts, plus the head. These babies were economical to produce and were very popular with children.

By 1910 the word "character" began to mean "realistic", and skillful, modeled realism were formed into the features of many dolls. Some of the larger heads were made in a smaller size by taking a mold cast of the fired head, which produced the same head, but considerably smaller. This same method used on the now smaller head, produced a yet smaller head, and so on. This method was common practice, but some smaller heads of particular mold numbers appear to be a remodeled version of the original, in fact some recognizable molds have had other features added, such as molded eyebrows, molded hair or dimples and this had to be accomplished by remodelled molds.

German bodies of the quality babies represent a baby or child in a natural position and each limb was individually modelled. The cheaper dolls have both arms and legs in the same positions, as it cost less for the molds.

A few words about Steiff: Prong marks were used until about 1972, now clips are riveted. About that same year they redesigned the tag eliminating the blue, so any tag with blue color is older. If no markings present look for "stitch" usually on the chest. Stitch was well fastened but children would pull tag from it. On the left ear, look through fur for any sign of prong mark. There are untagged authentic Steiff for even today in Stuttgart at the factory the rejects are sold, untagged. Earliest examples of Steiff are felt, although even into the 1950's and 1960's they combined mohair with felt. Mohair is still used on jointed Teddy Bears, but mostly animals are now made of draylon, etc. Short mohair extends into the 1960's, also. PEWTER ear clips with "FF" underscored are pre 1920. Steiff ears are always sewn on, never a cut slit into a straw head. As far as we know there is always a center seam on stomach and through magnification you can study the particular type thread used by Steiff. Some of the 1930's Steiff bears had a paper chest tag and some of the earlier animals had a paper tag attached with wire to a collar.

HOW TO USE THE PRICE GUIDE

Bisque dolls are gaged mainly by the quality of the head, both in the rarity of the mold and in the fineness of the bisque itself. The painting of the bisque should be flawless with no blotches, or white "scuff" marks, nor any pits, pock marks or black dots. The eye holes should be cut out in an even manner with both being near the same size. Many doll's heads were held in an upright position to cut one eye hole, then reversed upside down to cut the other side and sometimes the one eyehole will be "reversed" or enlarged.

Two, three or four dolls of the same mold can appear very different because of the quality of the artist's workmanship. Quality of bisque is actually a personal experience as some collectors do not object to "higher" color, while others prefer almost white bisque, with others liking pale pinkness, but the price of the doll should be reflected in this quality. A doll with "high" coloring (a later doll) such as S.F.B.J., Unis and many made after 1910 should not have as high a price (unless they are character dolls) as ones made earlier, with fine bisque.

Dolls prices have always been based on the bisque and body conditions, with the bisque being the most important factor. The body must be the correct one, French for a French head and German for a German head. If the head is a shoulder head it should be on a correct style body. For top dollar the doll should have an original, or appropriate body that is old and all in good condition. Minor damage, such as scuffs, a few paint flakes, chipped fingers or toes are minor, and a well repaired old body is much more desirable than a new body. Many of the later German dolls, especially the "character" bisque came on crude "stick" bodies or five piece, poor mache ones, but even if not liked, these have to be acceptable as original to the head. Some bodies actually denote the price of the dolls, such as a lady-type body, jointed toddler bodies, or some of the adorable tiny 8" and under bisque heads on fully jointed (even wrists, elbows and knees) bodies.

The quality of the bisque is of upmost importance in pricing a doll, and it is important that there are no breaks, hairline cracks, cracked or broken shoulder plates, eye chips, any mends or repairs at all, plus the QUALITY of the doll painting should be very, very good to excellent. If any doll is less than perfect the price should be less than for a perfect quality doll.

It is rare to find an old doll that has not been played with, mint and original, so the original clothes play no part in pricing for this book. If a doll has original wig and clothes, and is "mint", then a greater price should be asked for that special doll.

No matter what is said about prices, the collectors set their own prices by what they are willing to pay for a certain doll, plus they will pay more for dolls they are especially hunting for, or for the fine character dolls. If an individual, or dealer places too high a price on a doll it will most likely go unsold for a long time, and if the price is not reduced, the price will gain acceptance through the natural rate of inflation over a period of time.

Popularity of a certain doll moves prices up, for example the "Hilda" baby is so popular that the prices are based on that popularity and demand, and it is fortunate that the QUALITY of 99% of the "Hildas" is excellent, for there are a great many other babies with equal quality, charm, but not the popularity.

A scale method of pricing will be used to allow for the quality of the bisque (See next page).

VALUE GUIDE SCALE

A	.... $	50.00
B	....	100.00
C	....	150.00
D	....	200.00
E	....	250.00
F	....	300.00
G	....	350.00
H	....	400.00
I	....	450.00
J	....	500.00
K	....	600.00
L	....	700.00
M	....	800.00
N	....	900.00
O	....	1,000.00
P	....	1,050.00
Q	....	1,100.00
R	....	1,200.00
S	....	1,300.00
T	....	1,450.00
U	....	1,700.00
V	....	1,900.00
W	....	2,200.00
X	....	2,400.00
Y	....	2,700.00
Z	....	3,000.00
ZA	....	3,500.00
ZB	....	4,000.00
ZC	....	4,500.00
ZD	....	5,000.00
ZE	....	5,500.00
ZF	....	6,000.00
ZG	....	6,500.00
ZH	....	7,000.00
ZI	....	7,500.00
ZJ	....	8,000.00
ZK	....	8,500.00
ZL	....	9,000.00
ZM	....	9,500.00
ZN	....	10,000.00

Left to right: 36″ in old organdy dress and marked: Walkure-Germany-7½ (Kley & Hahn-registered in 1902). 40″ boy with original fur wig and marked: A.18 M. (Armand Marseille). 36″ marked: Walkure-Germany. (Kley and Hahn registered in 1902). Girls are courtesy of Irene Brown and boy, courtesy Josephine Wingfield.

36″ Walkure – M–N
36″ A.M. – L–M

Tea Party. Left to right: 33″ Spring strung and marked: N Made in Germany 17/164 (Kestner). 32″ marked: SH 1079 DEP 14½ (Simon & Halbig). 33″ marked: A.M. 390. (Armand Marseille). 33″ marked: 16 99 DEP Germany-Handwerck Halbig 7. (Made for Heinrich Handwerck by Simon & Halbig). All are open mouth with four teeth and on fully jointed composition bodies. Courtesy Irene Brown.

33″ 164 – L–M
32″ 1079 – L–M
33″ 99 – K–L

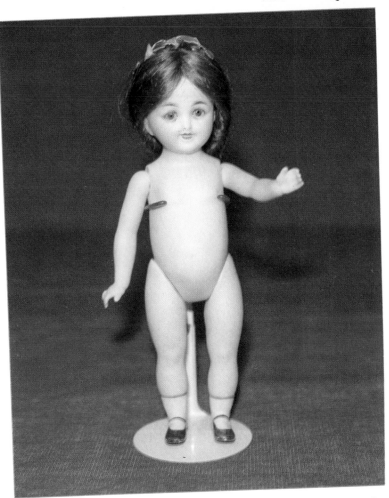

9″ All bisque with open/closed, smiling mouth with molded teeth. One piece body and head, molded on shoes and socks. Sleep eyes. Excellent quality. Courtesy Lilah Beck. Photo by Renie Culp.

9″ – F–G

5″ Excellent quality all bisque with open/closed mouth, set eyes and has molded on heeled boots. Courtesy Elaine Boyle.

5″ – C–D

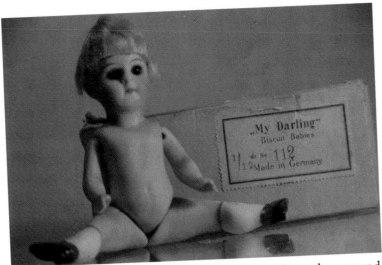

5½" "My Darling" all bisque with original box. Painted upper and lower lashes, brown sleep eyes and closed mouth. Molded on shoes that are brown and have two straps and a black pom pom. Marks: 154/5. Courtesy Diane Hoffman.

5½" – C-D

Left: All bisque that is 4¾" and marked: 130/3. Molded on brown double strap shoes and painted black bow. White painted stockings. One piece body and head and black pupiless sleep eyes. Value: C-D. Dog is 8" long and 6" high and is an early Steiff with up-prong marks. Cinnamon color felt, straw filled and glass eyes. Up-down toy on wheels (wood). Ca. before 1920. Value: A-B. Right: All bisque (on dog) is 4½" and marked: 520/2¼ with one piece body and head, painted blue eyes, molded on pink high boots, white stockings with blue trim. Value: A. Courtesy Margaret Mandel.

15

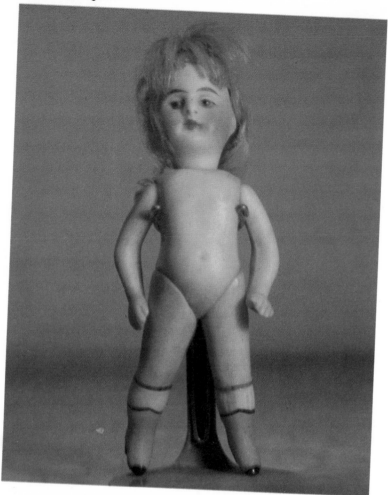

4″ All bisque with closed mouth and intaglio eyes (Painted and swivel neck). Molded on yellow painted boots. Courtesy Diane Hoffman.

4″ – E–F

5½″ All bisque Kestner twin marked: 833. Bent leg baby bodies, open/closed mouths and all original. Both have sleep eyes, but one has blue and other has brown. All original layette in original wicker basket. (Author).

Twins in basket – N–O
5½″ 833 baby alone – C–D

This 3½″ all bisque is molded all in one piece. It has excellent quality for a doll this size, therefore we are guessing that it was made in Germany. Molded blonde hair with hair bow. Courtesy Lilah Beck. Photo by Renie Culp.

3½″ – B–C

ALL BISQUE

5″ All bisque with molded tuff hair, painted eyes and watermelon mouth. All one piece except jointed at the shoulders. Courtesy Diane Hoffman.

5″ – A–C

5″ All bisque called "Cupid's Sister". Head molded in a turned position and is one piece with the body. Jointed at shoulders and hips. Watermelon mouth. Courtesy Diane Hoffman.

5″ – A–C

4½″ German all bisque with painted eyes looking to side. Large feet with painted shoes and socks. Has original leather boxing gloves. Marks: P.46/three leaf clover/- Made in Germany. Courtesy Josephine Wingfield.

4½″ – A–B

28″ Beautiful doll marked: Made in Germany/Armand Marseille/390n/DRGM 21/A.12M. Human hair wig. Doll bought in England. Courtesy Barbara Earnshaw.

10″ – B–C
14″ – B–C
16″ – C–D
18″ – C–D
24″ – D–E
28″ – F–G

ARMAND MARSEILLE

31" Bisque head with open mouth and marked: Walkure. The baby has an 18" bisque head with open mouth marked: Germany/-G.327 B./D.R.G.M. 259/A.9.M. Courtesy Barbara Earnshaw.

14" – C–D
16" – D–E
20" – E–F
24" – H–I
31" – K–L

17" Bisque socket head on stick type, ball jointed body. Redressed in old clothes. Brown set eyes, open mouth with teeth. Mold number 1894/A.M. 11" early bear with greenish gold mohair, straw filled, fully jointed, flat footed with felt pads, glass eyes. Steiff before 1910. Value: C–D. 9" Schuco (German) monkey, manipulate the tail to move the head to say "yes or no". Brown mohair and felt, fully jointed, glass eyes. Value: A–B. 15" Schuco YES-NO monkey dressed as organ grinder, felt and mohair, fully jointed, clothes are sewn on. Value: A–B. All courtesy Margaret Mandel.

14" – C–E
17" – E–F
24" – F–G
28" – G–H

14" "Baby Betty". Socket head on ball jointed body with straight wrists. Sleep eyes, open mouth with four teeth and mohair wig. Original navy dress with white pinafore and bonnet. Marks: A./Baby 3/Ox/Betty (in circle)/M. Courtesy Irene Brown.

$$
\begin{array}{rl}
14" & - \text{C–D} \\
17" & - \text{D–E} \\
20" & - \text{E–F} \\
26" & - \text{F–G}
\end{array}
$$

ARMAND MARSEILLE

7" Painted bisque socket head on five piece composition body. Googly eyes to side. All original clothes. Some of these 7" sizes were dressed by the founder of the Vogue Doll Co. Marks: Just Me/A 310 M. Also came in 10" and 12" sizes. Courtesy Diane Hoffman.

7" – E–F
7" Fired in color – L–M

10" Painted bisque that is all original with first known Vogue Doll Co. tag that is white with gold lettering and says: Vogue. Composition body, sleep blue eyes and right arm is bent at elbow. Doll is marked: Just Me/Registered/Germany/A. 310/7/O M. (Armand Marseille). Courtesy Barbara Boury.

10" – F–G
10" Fired in color – N–O

All original Flapper that is 17″ tall and marked: Armand
Marseille/390/Germany/A. 1½ M. Standing next to Victorian
Doll House of 1917 from the Jerry Smith Collection. Built by an Ar-
chitect for his daughter. Courtesy Barbara Earnshaw.

17″ Flapper body – E–F

ARMAND MARSEILLE

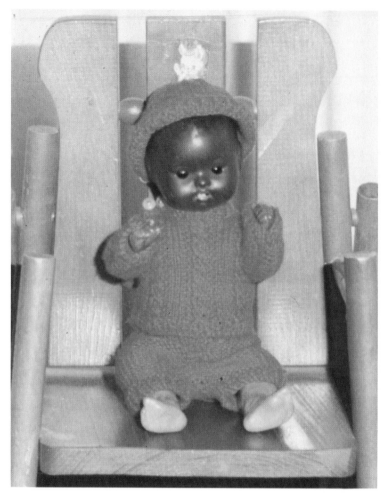

10" Black "My Dream Baby" made by Armand Marseille for the Arranbee Doll Co. Bent leg baby body, open mouth and sleep eyes. Marks: A.M. 351 Germany. Courtesy Olive Krol. Photo by Rita Johnson.

10" White – C–D; Black – D–E
12" White – D–E; Black – E–F
18" White – F–G; Black – G–H

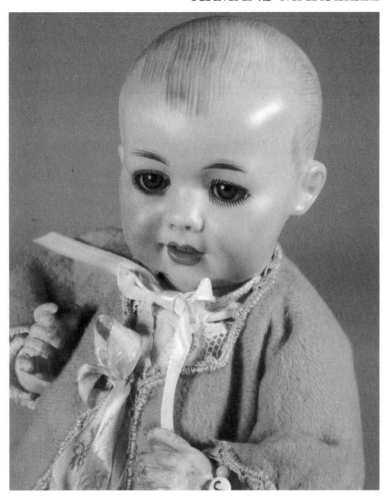

14″ Very beautiful bisque socket head on five piece composition, bent leg baby body. Sleep blue eyes, open mouth with two lower teeth. Brush painted hair on a solid dome. Marks: Germany/ G 326 B/A.A.M./D.R.G.M. 250. Dorothy Coleman suggests that the "G.B." may stand for Gabriel Brenda instead of George Borgfeldt. (Author).

14″ – E–F

ARRANBEE

10½″ Head circumference, flange neck baby on cloth body that has bent limbs and celluloid hands. The right hand has a molded celluloid bottle and the arm is spring strung so that it always goes to the mouth. The mouth is open with two teeth. Sleep eyes with painted lashes above and below. Hair is molded and faintly painted. Clothes are probably original. Head marked: Germany/Arranbee. Bottle: Arranbee Pat. Aug. 10-'26. Courtesy Irene Brown.

10½″ – D–E

16″ Head circumference baby on five piece bent limb baby body and marked: B ⤬ & P / 604/16. Brown eyes with painted lashes above and below, open mouth with two teeth and tongue. Owner's other twin grand-daughter borrowed this outfit for her own Christening. Made by Bahr & Proschild. Courtesy Irene Brown.

12″ – D–E
16″ – F–G
20″ – H–I

BERGMANN, C.M.

19″ Marked: C.M. Bergman/Simon & Halbig/7. Blue sleep eyes with lashes and on fully jointed composition body. Pierced ears and original mohair wig. Her dress is white organdy with lots of lace and pink ribbons are silk. The shoes are soft pink leather with a feather decoration on toes and all her clothes are original. Head made by Simon & Halbig for C.M. Bergmann. Courtesy Barbara Boury.

19″ Re-dressed – E–F
19″ Original – G–H

15" Bisque socket head on five piece bent leg baby body. Solid dome with original caracul wig. Open/closed mouth with molded tongue, brown sleep eyes and marked: Simon & Halbig/C.M. Bergmann/Made in Germany/615-6. The head was made for Bergmann by Simon and Halbig. Courtesy Penny Pendlebury. Photo by Chuck.

12" – D–E
16" – F–G
20" – H–I

15" Boy and girl to show the original costume on the girl. See close up of the boy's head on following page. Both made by Catterfelder Puppenfabrik. Courtesy Barbara Earnshaw.

15" Boy – T–U
15" Girl – S–T

15" All original and rare character girl marked: CP 215. Bisque head on fully jointed composition body. Large painted blue eyes and fully closed mouth. Courtesy Barbara Earnshaw.

15" – S–T

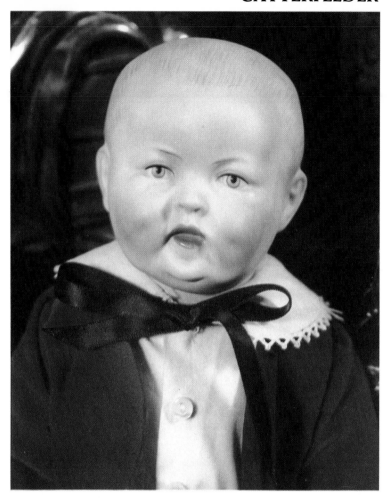

15″ Rare character boy marked: CP201. Bisque head on fully jointed composition body. Intaglio blue painted eyes and wide open/closed mouth. Courtesy Barbara Earnshaw.

15″ – T-U

DRESSEL, C & D

14½" Lady by Cuno & Otto Dressel, on composition ball jointed adult body. Sleep eyes and closed mouth. Original wig with braids. Marks: 1669/C & O D/Germany 12. Courtesy Josephine Wingfield.

14½" – J-K

Close-up of Lady by Cuno & Otto Dressel.

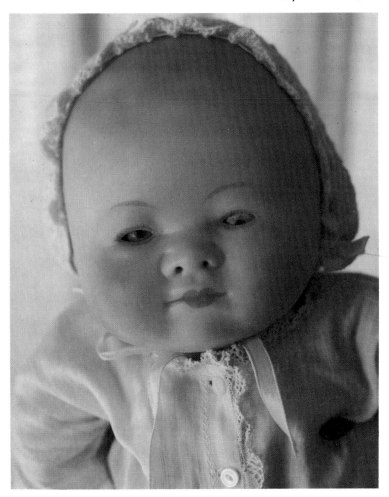

12″ Head circumference bisque with odd shaped head with
wrinkles molded on back of neck. Pierced nostrils, brown sleep
eyes with tiny lashes painted above and below the eyes. Cloth body
with composition hands and the right hand is almost clenched.
Marks: 3 Arthur A. Gerling. Flange neck. Courtesy Irene Brown.

12″ – E–F
16″ – F–G
20″ – H–I

GOEBEL

10" Character child made by Goebel. She has extremely round eyes, open mouth with two upper teeth and is on a five piece, bent leg baby body. Marks: /B5/Germany. Courtesy Josephine Wingfield.

W G

10" – C–D

24″ Bisque head that is incised Handwerck Halbig. Ball jointed body, brown sleep eyes, painted lashes top and bottom, open mouth/teeth. Dress hand made by owner's mother at age 12 in 1913. Value: F–G. The 22″ bear on rubber wheels (far left) is all straw stuffed, early cotton plush with glass eyes. Value: D–E. 22″ Bear on right with cast iron wheels is early long mohair that suggests Steiff as the maker, all straw filled, glass eyes. Value: F–G. Courtesy Margaret Mandel.

6″ Tall brass head marked: DRGM 160638, on front shoulder and Diana/7 DEP, in square, on back. Four sew holes, molded and painted hair, glass eyes, open mouth with four teeth. In original box marked: Diana Metal heads. Made by Alfred Heller in 1903. Courtesy Irene Brown.

6″ Head – A–B
23″ Doll – C–D

HORSMAN
HEUBACH, GEBRUDER

15" "Tynie Baby" made by Horsman in 1924. Bisque head with sleep eyes and a puckered frown. Closed mouth. Cloth body with celluloid hands. Designed by Bernard Lipfert. Some came with composition hands and heads, also some hands were rubber. Courtesy Barbara Earnshaw.

15" – I-J

7½" Bisque head, intaglio eyed googly with molded tuffed hair. Five piece papier mache body. All original. Marks: 3/Od 90, Heubach in square 85. Courtesy Barbara Earnshaw.

7½" – C-D

7" Glass eye googly marked Heubach, in a square, 5/0. Crude five piece papier mache body and closed "watermelon" mouth. Courtesy Barbara Earnshaw.

7" – X–Z

"Dolly Dimples" by Heubach and so incised. Brown sleep eyes, open mouth and deep cheek dimples. The body is composition and fully jointed. Courtesy Elizabeth Burke.

19" – S–T
23" – U–V

22″ Bisque socket head on fully jointed body. Glass sleep eyes and closed mouth with cheek dimples. Marks: ?-number- 407/8/- Germany. A possible Heubach little girl of ca. 1910. All original clothes and hair ribbon. Courtesy Barbara Earnshaw.

16″ – P–Q
22″ – U–V

HEUBACH, GEBRUDER

Character Heubach with sunburst mark and mold number 8192. Unusual open mouth smiling little girl that has a long, slender nose. On fully jointed composition body. Courtesy Elizabeth Burke.

14" – E–F
17" – G–H
21" – H–I

Heubach character "pouty" incised with the number 6970. Sleep eyes and closed pouty mouth. Body is fully jointed and of composition. Courtesy Elizabeth Burke.

14″ – S–T
17″ – U–V
21″ – V–W

HEUBACH, GEBRUDER

18″ Toddler Gebruder Heubach that is marked with the "sunburst" mark. Original wig, glass eyes and an open/closed mouth with molded teeth. Courtesy Elaine Boyle.

$$12″ - G-H$$
$$16″ - M-O$$
$$18″ - O-Q$$
$$21″ - R-T$$

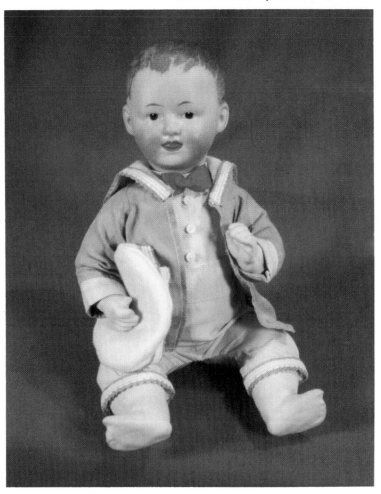

9½" Heubach boy. Bent limb composition baby body with separate, and protruding large toes. Black intaglio eyes with tiny white dots at top of lid. Open/closed mouth with molded tongue and teeth. Flocked hair. Wears original old suit, no shoes. Marks: 85 78/ Heubach, in square/ 76 (green stamp) 23. Courtesy Irene Brown.

9½" – E-F
13" – G-H

HEUBACH, GEBRUDER

10" Heubach girl on ball jointed composition body. Blue sleep eyes, closed pouty mouth and original blonde mohair wig. Clothes are old and may be original. Marks: 7247/Germany/2 [HEU BACH] /22 (Green stamp). Courtesy Irene Brown.

10" – K–L
14" – S–T
16" – U–V

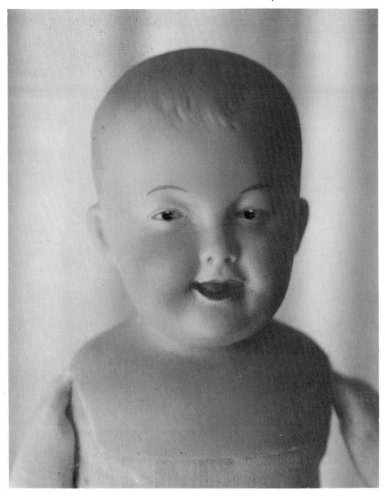

11½" Bisque shoulder head on straw stuffed body. Composition arms and legs. Open/closed mouth with molded tongue. Intaglio black eyes with white highlight dots at top. Molded and painted hair. Marks: 76 [HEU BACH] 44/ DEP/Germany. Courtesy Irene Brown.

$$11\frac{1}{2}" - F-G$$
$$13" - G-H$$
$$16" - I-J$$

HEUBACH, KOPPLESDORF

A very rare LARGE size black bisque with 15″ head circumference with overall height of 19″. Marks: Heubach-Kopplesdorf/399-4 DRGM/Germany. Solid dome head with black curly wig, brown glass eyes with red dots in corners and nostrils, closed mouth and full painted lips. Bent leg composition body. Has sticker on stomach that says: "Bermuda". Pierced ears. Courtesy Irene Brown.

12″ – G–H
16″ – I–J
19″ – K–L

Black bisque mother doll with baby, which came as a set. Heubach Kopplesdorf/399-16/0, on mother, and the baby is marked with mold number 396. 19/0. The mother is 9½" with glass eyes and composition body. The baby is 5" with painted eyes and cotton stuffed body with composition arms. Original earrings. Courtesy Josephine Wingfield.

9½" & 5" Set – J-K

HEUBACH, KOPPLESDORF

14" Heubach Kopplesdorf baby on five piece, bent leg baby body.
Blue sleep eyes, open mouth with two teeth. Marks: 321/40/Germany. Courtesy Penny Pendlebury. Photo by Chuck.

14" – D–E
20" – H–I

HEUBACH, KOPPLESDORF

18" Bisque head on five piece bent leg baby body. Brown sleep eyes, open mouth with upper teeth, dimples in cheeks and chin and moving tongue. Marks: Heubach-Kopplesdorf/300-4. Courtesy Gloyra Woods.

18" – G-H

15" Head circumference Heubach Kopplesdorf baby marked 2678 D.R.G.M. Original mohair wig, moveable tongue in open mouth, brown sleep eyes and on five piece bent leg baby body. Wearing old Christening dress borrowed from the doll for the Christening of owner's twin granddaughters. Courtesy Irene Brown.

16" – E-F
18" – G-H
24" – I-J

49

28″ Painted bisque with brown flirty eyes and fur lashes. Open mouth with two teeth. Cryer in five piece composition bent leg baby body. Marks: Heubach Kopplesdorf/342.9. Germany. Courtesy Cheryl Pendlebury and photo by Chuck Pendlebury.

16″ – B–C
18″ – D–E
21″ – F–G
28″ – H–I

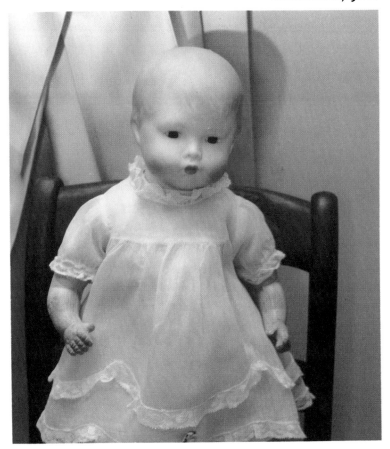

20″ Rare "Baby Bo Kay", cloth body, composition legs and arms, with bisque head. Molded blonde hair. All original and head marked: Copr. by J.L. Kallus/Germany. Courtesy Barbara Earnshaw.

16″ – U–V
20″ – Y–Z

KAMMER & RINEHARDT

22" Bisque head with sleep brown eyes and open mouth. Marks: Simon Halbig/K star R/ 55. Head made by Simon & Halbig for Kammer & Reinhardt. Courtesy Barbara Earnshaw.

22" – F–G

KAMMER & RINEHARDT

15" Toddler that is marked: K star R/115A. Pouty closed mouth, sleep eyes and molded hair. Also comes on a five piece, bent leg baby body. Courtesy Elaine Boyle.

15" – T–U
23" – V–W

25" Bisque head on five piece bent leg baby body. Brown sleep eyes. Open/-closed mouth and original mohair wig. Marks: K star R/-Simon & Halbig/116-/A. Head made for Kammer and Rine-hardt by Simon and Halbig. Courtesy O.D. Gregg.

15" – S–T
22" – U–V
25" – V–W

53

KAMMER & RINEHARDT

20″ Marked: K star R 117A (Mein Leibling) has brown sleep eyes and her big brother marked K star R 116A has blue sleep eyes. She has full closed mouth and he has open/closed mouth. Girl dressed by Shirley Jones and both courtesy Cathy Turchan.

20″ – W–X
24″ 117A–Y–Z
22″ 116A–U–V

26" Bisque head with flirty eyes and lashes. Open mouth with four teeth, mohair wig and original German made crocheted dress and cap. She wears an original garter belt to hold up stockings. Her body is a "flapper" type with joint above knee for shorter dresses worn then. Marks: K star R/Simon Halbig/117n-/Germany/65. Courtesy Irene Brown.

18" – H-I
22" – I-J
26" – J-K

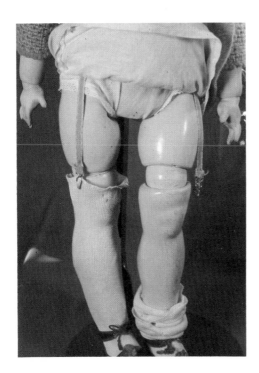

Shows the position of the knee joints on a "flapper" body and the original garter belt and stockings. Courtesy Irene Brown.

18" Not flapper body
    – F–G
22" Not flapper body
    – G–H
26" Not flapper body
    – I–J

KAMMER & RINEHARDT

22½" Bisque head with closed mouth and sleep eyes marked: K star R/Simon-Halbig/117. Kammer and Rinehardt doll with head made by Simon and Halbig. Holding 12" baby marked Hilda. (Made by Kestner). Both courtesy Barbara Earnshaw.

22½" 117 – W–X
12" Hilda – M–N

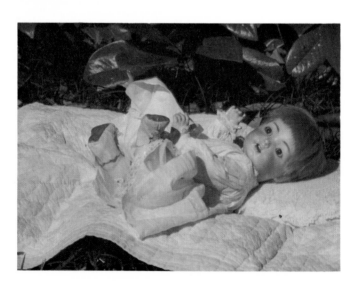

18" Bisque socket head baby on five piece bent leg body. Open mouth, dimples and sleep eyes. Marks: K star R/122. Courtesy Elaine Boyle.

14" – G–H
18" – H–I
22" – I–J

56

30″ Kammer and Rinehardt with bisque head, and on fully jointed composition body. Open mouth and brown sleep eyes, molded eyebrows with painted lashes top and bottom. Pierced ears. Marks: Halbig/K star R/76. Doll made by Kammer and Reinhardt, using a head made by Simon and Halbig. Value: J–K. Shown also are two Steiff animals. 25″ sitting tiger, all straw stuffing, mohair and open felt mouth with wood teeth. Value: D–E. 13″ Lion cub, fully jointed, early mohair and all straw stuffed. Value: A–B. Courtesy Margaret Mandel.

22″ Bisque head marked: K star R 121 Germany/S & H. Made by Simon and Halbig for Kammer and Reinhardt. Mohair wig, blue sleep eyes, open mouth with two teeth and dimples and moving tongue. On bent leg baby body. Courtesy Gloyra Woods.

    14″ – G-H
    22″ – I-J
    26″ – K-L

KAMMER & RINEHARDT

16″ All original bent leg baby marked: K star R/Simon Halbig/121. Excellent quality clothes that includes a rattle. A 4th Place Winner, National Convention, Denver 1978. Head made by Simon and Halbig for Kammer and Rinehardt. Courtesy Barbara Earnshaw.

16″ – G–H

13″ With 10″ head circumference. Brown sleep eyes with special mechanism that keeps eyes from sleeping until released. Called, "Naughty Baby" in old ads. Bent leg composition baby body, open mouth with two teeth, and strawberry blonde mohair wig. Dressed in old hand knit suit with organdy bonnet. The big toes protrude. Marks: K Star R/Simon & Halbig/Germany/126/32. Head made by Simon & Halbig for Kammer and Reinhardt. Courtesy Irene Brown.

13″ – G–H

KAMMER & RINEHARDT

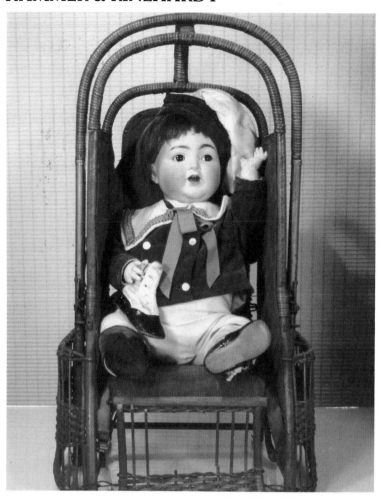

Very large 24″ K star R/Simon Halbig/Germany/126-62 bought in England by owner Barbara Earnshaw. Head made by Simon & Halbig for Kammer & Reinhardt. Flirty sleep brown eyes and open mouth with movable tongue. Carrier is a back pack and wicker, also purchased in England.

$$14″ - G-H$$
$$18 - H-I$$
$$22″ - I-J$$
$$24″ - J-K$$

24″ Bisque head on bent leg, five piece baby body. Human hair wig, brown sleep eyes, open mouth with two teeth, moving tongue and marked: K star R/Simon & Halbig/126. Head made by Simon & Halbig for Kammer and Reinhardt. Courtesy Gloyra Woods.

24″ – J–K

Very large 28″ tall character baby with head made by Simon and Halbig for Kammer and Rinehardt, and head circumference of 19″. Mold number 128. Courtesy Josephine Wingfield.

14″ – G–H
18″ – H–I
22″ – I–J
24″ – J–K
28″ – M–N

KAMMER & RINEHARDT

15″ Celluloid "Marie". Kid body, painted eyes, closed pouty mouth and braided mohair wig in "buns" over the ears. Original peasant dress. Celluloid version of the 101 pouty marked: K star R/301. Courtesy Irene Brown.

11″ Celluloid head – H–I
15″ Celluloid head – L–M
11″ Bisque head – R–S
15″ Bisque head – U–V

Two Kestners that are 17″ and 12″. Both have open mouths, are characters and on ball jointed bodies. The 17″ one is marked: Made in G Germany 11 and the 12″: Made in A Germany 5. Courtesy Betty Shelley.

12″ – C–D
17″ – F–G

14" Kestner with interchangeable heads. All are bisque and the body is a fully jointed composition one. Box is marked: Kestner Character. Head on body marked: 184. Other heads marked: 178-top, 175-middle and 185-bottom. Original chemise on doll. Courtesy Barbara Earnshaw.

14" Set – Z–ZA
14" Doll only. Closed mouth – L–M
14" Doll only. Open mouth. – D–E

28″ Closed mouth Kestner marked: L 15/128/Made in Germany. Brown sleep eyes and on fully jointed composition body. Clothes are all original. She has a pouty expression. Courtesy Cathy Turchan.

    14″ – J–K
    20″ – M–N
    28″ – Q–R

KESTNER

18″ Early Kestner with closed mouth. Marks: X1, on upper part of head. Wrists not jointed. Composition body. Courtesy Josephine Wingfield.

14″ – J–K
18″ – L–M
21″ – M–N

21" Closed mouth bisque head on fully jointed composition body. Set blue eyes, original. Marks: 14, on head. Most likely made by Kestner. (Author).

14" – J-K
17" – L-M
21" – M-N

28" Closed mouth bisque head with deep shoulder plate. Original kid body is pin jointed at hips and she has bisque lower arms. Set gray-blue paperweight eyes, painted lashes top and bottom and decal eyebrows. Sharply pointed nose and deep red liner at lip separation. Deeply incised between nostrils to lip and a deep crown slice with high forehead. 13" head circumference. Mark on shoulder plate: 698/12. 8" Steiff lamb (prong marks) that is all straw and has green glass eyes. 26" Steiff lion with straw head and straw & kapok body and limbs. All Courtesy Margaret Mandel.

28" 698 – M–N
Lamb – A
Lion – D–E

Closer look at the doll marked 698. She was most likely an early doll made by Kestner for Jumeau.

22" Kestner mold #154 with bisque head, sleep brown eyes, painted lashes top and bottom, molded eyebrows, open mouth with molded teeth. Kid body with bisque lower arms. Has Universal knee joint and Ne Plus Ultra hip joints, original blonde mohair wig and has been redressed in old clothes. Value: H-I. 25" black and white mohair dog with original red bow, brown glass eyes and made as a pajama bag. Label: "Merry Thought, Ironbridge Shops, Made in England. Reg'd Design. Value: A-B. 10" Steiff Siamese cat of mohair, all straw filled and pointed at neck only, is in sitting position, has open, pink felt mouth, pink felt ears with ear clip. Label: Made in Western Germany. Ca. late 1940's. Value: A-B. Courtesy Margaret Mandel.

Shows a closer view of the Kestner 154. Courtesy Margaret Mandel.

10" All original bisque head, button nose googly. Head is marked: 241, possibly a Kestner. Courtesy Barbara Earnshaw.

10" – X–Y
12" – Z–ZA

21" "Gibson Girl" made by J.D. Kestner and marked: 172-7. Sleep eyes/lashes, closed mouth and all original. Courtesy Barbara Earnshaw.

21" – L–M

12″ Kestner mold number 143 with open mouth and sleep eyes. Bisque head on fully jointed composition body. All original. Courtesy Barbara Earnshaw.

> 12″ – C–D
> 16″ – E–F
> 20″ – F–G

16″ With open/closed mouth and marked: 151 (Kestner). He has very pale bisque and high color in cheeks. Set grey eyes. Courtesy Cathy Turchan.

14″ – F–G
16″ – G–H
18″ – H–I

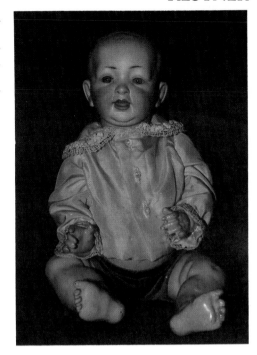

20″ "Baby Jean" bisque head marked only J.D.K. Brush stroke hair painted on a solid dome, sleep eyes, open mouth and dimpled cheeks. Chubby baby body. Courtesy Gloyra Woods.

16″ – G–H
20″ – H–I

KESTNER

20″ Bisque socket head on five piece bent leg baby body. Light blue, almost grey, sleep eyes, open mouth. Marks: 152/-11. Made by Kestner. Courtesy Diane Hoffman.

20″ – I-J

16″ Bisque head baby on bent leg body and all original. Head is bisque and marked: 152-6½. Originally in the reknown Jerry Smith collection. Sleep eyes and open mouth. Made by Kestner. Courtesy Barbara Earnshaw.

16″ – F-G

20″ – I-J

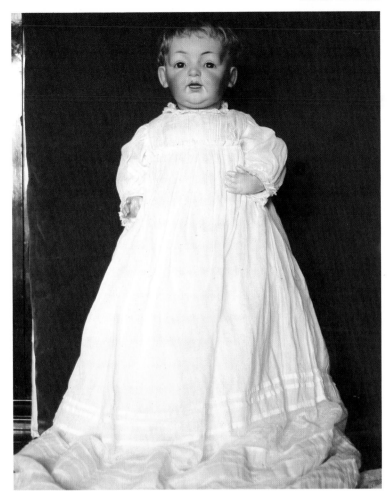

19" Bisque head on five piece, bent leg baby body and marked: JDK/ K 14/Made in Germany/211. He has open/closed mouth, mohair wig and elaborate Christening clothes are original. Courtesy Cathy Turchan.

14" – E–F
19" – I–J
23" – J–K

KESTNER

16" Kestner 211 mold number baby with open mouth and on a five piece, bent leg baby body. Original wig and clothes. Courtesy Olive Krol. Photo by Rita Johnson.

16" – G-H

18" Head circumference large JDK 211 baby. Brown sleep eyes with painted upper and lower lashes. Open mouth with two lower teeth. Doll in lap is marked: Nippon. Courtesy Diane Hoffman.

16" – G-H
20" – I-J
26" – K-L

30" Bisque head on fully jointed composition body. Open mouth and molded eyebrows. Marks: Made in Germany/J.D.K./214. Courtesy Mary Sweeney.

$$
\begin{aligned}
16" &- E\text{-}F \\
21" &- F\text{-}G \\
26" &- J\text{-}K \\
30" &- K\text{-}L
\end{aligned}
$$

11½" "Little William" by J.D. Kestner and marked: 238 JDK/Germany. Open/closed mouth, blue eyes and blonde mohair wig. Kid body marked with Crown and Streamers (JDK-Germany) ½ cork stuffed. Bisque lower arms. Original clothes. Courtesy Irene Brown.

11½" – E–F
14" – F–G

21" Bisque head baby that is marked just with the J.D.K. and a size number, and referred to by collectors as "Baby Jean". There is a different likeness to the "Hilda". Five piece, bent leg baby body. Courtesy Elaine Boyle.

17" – G–H
21" – H–I

12" Fired in brown bisque head on matching brown composition, fully jointed body. Open mouth with four upper teeth, sleep eyes. Marks: (incised) 6 Germany 240. Courtesy Terri Weston.

12" – D–E
16" – G–H
21" – I–J

21" (Wigged) and 19" (Bald head) Hilda. Both are on the typical "Hilda" five piece, bent leg baby body, have open mouths and blue sleep eyes. Bald head with brush stroke, molded hair is marked: J.D.K./Ges.Gesch/1070/Made in Germany. The one with wig is marked: 245/J.D.K. Jr./1914/Hilda/Made in Germany. Wigged: Courtesy Elaine Boyle. Bald. Courtesy Author.

18" – T–U
21" – V–W

16″ Bisque head with flirty eyes, open mouth with two upper teeth, original peach organdy dress, slip and bonnet. Bent leg baby body. Marks: J.D.K./257. Courtesy Gloyra Woods.

16″ – F–G

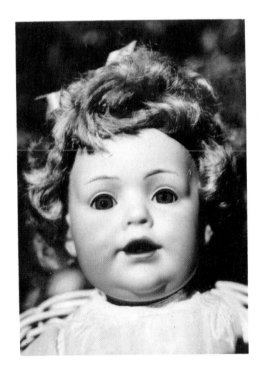

17″ Bisque head marked: J.D.K./247. Human hair wig, blue sleep eyes, open mouth with upper teeth and dimples in cheeks. Bent leg baby body. Courtesy Gloyra Woods.

17″ – F–G

KESTNER

19" Bisque head with open mouth and two upper teeth, brown sleep eyes, mohair wig. Bent leg baby body. Marks: J.D.K. 257. Courtesy Gloyra Woods.

19" – G–H

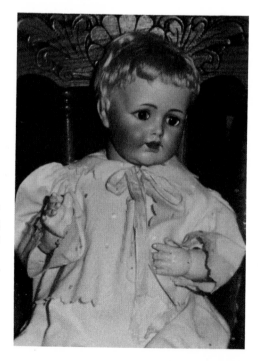

20" Bisque head baby on five piece, bent leg baby body. Open mouth and sleep eyes, original wig and clothes. Marks: J.D.K. 257. Courtesy Olive Krol. Photo by Rita Johnson.

20" – G–H

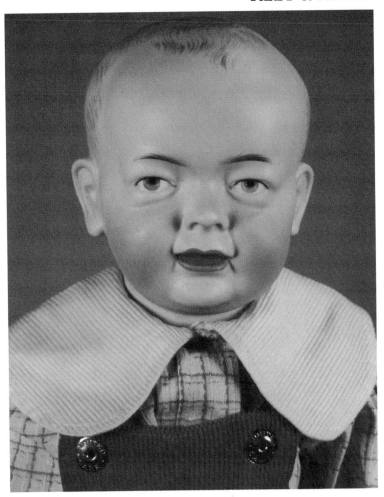

18″ Kley and Hahn bisque head boy on fully jointed composition body. Open/closed mouth with intaglio brown painted eyes. Brush stroke hair. Marks: K & H, in banner and 523. (Author).

18″ – N–O

15½" Kley and Hahn character boy with intaglio eyes and brush painted hair marked: 110. Old Teddy rides with him on a 1910's wood Studabaker horse drawn wagon. Courtesy Barbara Earnshaw.

15½" – M–N
18" – N–O

21″ Bisque head marked K & H and made by Kley and Hahn. Mohair wig, blue sleep eyes, dimples at corners of mouth and a very different double chin. She is on a ball jointed toddler body. Courtesy Gloyra Woods.

21″ – G-H

Bisque head baby with 10″ head circumference. Brush stroke painted hair, brown painted eyes and open/closed mouth with two upper teeth and tongue molded in. Five piece bent leg baby body with right leg extended and left leg sharply bent. Marks: ≥K & H≤- Germany/158-4. Courtesy Irene Brown.

22″ – G-H

KNOCH, GEBRUDER
MAKER UNKNOWN

10″ Gebruder Knoch with bisque socket head, open mouth, dimples and a smile. Sleep brown eyes and on a five piece bent leg baby body. Marks: 199 4/0. A very cute character baby. Courtesy Penny Pendlebury and photo by Chuck.

10″ – A–B
14″ – C–D
17″ – E–F

10″ Tall with 8″ head circumference. Open/closed mouth with molded tongue and upper teeth. Double chin, cheek dimples, and painted upper and lower lashes. Bent leg baby body of composition. Wearing hand crocheted jacket and cap. Marks: 2/0 151. Maybe made by Kestner. Courtesy Irene Brown.

10″ – C–D
14″ – F–G

22″ Character toddler that is incised: B-7. Molded hair, molded smiling mouth that is open/closed and has molded teeth. Original clothes. Courtesy Elaine Boyle.

13″ – G–H

22″ – R–T

MAKER UNKNOWN

12″ Boy marked: 400/0. Body is ball jointed with early straight wrists and the bisque head has an open mouth with teeth. Set glass eyes and is wearing his original sailor suit. Courtesy Irene Brown.

12″ – G–H
20″ – R–T

18½ " Shoulder head on kid body that is marked: 7½, high on head. Closed mouth. Her bisque is very pale and she has threaded paperweight set eyes. Her blonde mohair wig and clothes are original. She may be a Kestner. Courtesy Cathy Turchan.

14" – K-L
18" – L-M
24" – N-O

MAKER UNKNOWN

14" Bisque head on French composition and wood body with straight wrists. Large sleep eyes, open closed mouth with molded tongue and teeth. Original mohair wig. These dolls are marked only with a size number. It would be nice to try to make a "French" doll out of this style doll, but in most cases they were made in Germany. (Author).

14" – K–L
17" – L–M

19" Bisque head on fully jointed composition body. Blue sleep eyes with painted and hair lashes, open mouth and four teeth. Chin dimple. Dressed in old Greek costume. Human hair wig styled with buns over the ears. Marks: 1., on head. Maker uncertain. Courtesy Irene Brown.

19" G–H

18½" Bisque shoulder head with solid dome that has one hole, brown paperweight eyes, closed mouth and painted upper and lower lashes. Has accent line between lips. French style gusseted kid body with bisque lower arms. Marks: 7, on shoulder plate. Replaced wig and clothes. Courtesy Margaret Mandel.

14" – K–L
18" – L–M
23" – N–O

MAKER UNKNOWN

17" Unmarked doll in original clothes and original box bottom only. The doll has replaced arms and legs. Turned head with closed mouth and painted upper and lower lashes. High forehead with open dome and ears are not pierced. Set blue eyes. Maker may have been Kestner. Courtesy Diane Hoffman.

17" – J–K

A closer look at the detail and excellent quality of the bisque on the turned head, closed mouth doll. Courtesy Diane Hoffman.

26″ Bisque turned shoulder head with full closed mouth and set eyes. Kid body with bisque lower arms. All original clothes and wig. Courtesy Barbara Earnshaw.

15″ – I-J
18″ – J-K
22″ – K-L
26″ – L-M

MAKER UNKNOWN

14" Bisque head with open mouth and rare double row of teeth with lower teeth and tongue that retract when the doll is laying down to "sleep". Bent leg composition baby body. Redressed in old fabrics. Sleep eyes and mohair wig. Marks: 410/3. Courtesy Irene Brown.

14" – I-J

18" Marked: 8, high on head. Composition body has "Mama" and "Papa" pull strings and is very unusual, all ball joints are attached to lower limbs except at shoulder. She has straight wrists and is able to kneel and assume almost any position. Blue sleep eyes and fingers are all molded together. Closed mouth. Courtesy Cathy Turchan.

94   18" – L-M

15″ Tall with 11″ head circumference. Bisque head with molded and brushed marked hair, painted blue eyes with white highlights on pupil, lined in black above and also red eyeliner. Open/closed mouth with molded tongue. Dimple in double chin and above lips. Marks: 12. Courtesy Irene Brown.

15″ – F–G

13½″ Head circumference. Bisque head with molded and painted brush stroke hair, sleep eyes with painted lashes over and under eyes. Two cheek dimples, double chin, open mouth with molded teeth and tongue. Large ears. 16″ tall on five piece bent leg baby body. In long batiste dress, flannel slip, wool sacque and cap. Marks: 3-10. Courtesy Irene Brown.

16″ – G–H

MAKER UNKNOWN

12" Bisque head with intaglio eyes, open/-closed mouth with molded teeth. Brush stroke painted hair on solid dome. Marked only with 115, and on a French ball jointed body with straight wrists. He looks either Heubach or Kley and Hahn. Courtesy Betty Shelly.

12" – I-J
16" – K-L
20" – L-M

12" Unknown bisque head baby on cloth body with composition hands. Character face with closed, pouty mouth and sleep eyes. Hair is modeled and painted. Marks: #0 Made in Germany. Courtesy Barbara Earnshaw.

12" – I-J

19" Turned head marked with an "H", high on crown. Original white lawn dress. Painted upper and lower lashes, open mouth, brown sleep eyes, cloth body with composition arms with straight wrists. Courtesy Diane Hoffman.

19" – J–K

24" Bisque head on fully jointed composition body. Open mouth and only marked G.B. (George Borgfeldt or Gabriel Brenda). This doll was rescued from a dump in 1929 and restored by restringing. Original human hair wig. Her dress has old lace found at an estate sale. Owned and dressed by Shirley Derr.

24" – G–H

12″ Heubach mechanical girl pushing chair and Teddy Bear. Set eyes and open/closed mouth. All original except wig. Companion piece on following page. Courtesy Barbara Earnshaw.

12″ – Z–ZA

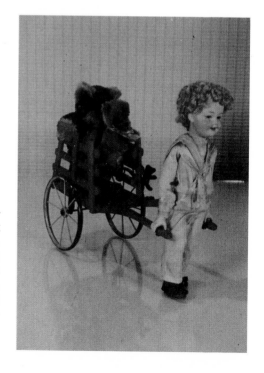

12″ Companion mechanical boy pulling cart of Teddy Bears. Made by Heubach with heads marked: Heubach 1/Germany. All original except wig. Courtesy Barbara Earnshaw.

12″ – Z–ZA

Close up of Heubach head on mechanicals with Teddy Bears.
Courtesy Barbara Earnshaw.

Victorian era wicker buggy. Courtesy Roberta Lago. Photo by Ted Long.

G–H

Steiff display ark. Tip to tip across the top measures 34½" and across the bottom 28" and width across the center is 12". Trees are removable, as is the house. Stamped: Made in Germany. Courtesy Martha Gragg.

N–O

A beautiful wicker buggy holding an 18″ Black German baby. (A.M.). Courtesy Roberta Lago. Photo by Ted Long.

G–H

12″ tall piano baby of bisque and marked only with an "A" and blue stamped Germany, on the bottom. Molded hair and painted blue eyes, holding a 4″ baby. It is not known for certain if this piano baby is a reproduction, as a great many of this type have been reproduced, with some marked: Taiwan. Caution is advised before paying a large amount for any piano baby. Courtesy Penny Pendlebury. Photo by Chuck.

Old – G–H

New – A

6" Doll House doll with good detail. Blue painted eyes, molded breast plate. Pink bisque head with white bisque arms and legs. Came in sets of the whole family and most difficult to find are the Grandma & Pa. Courtesy Diane Hoffman.

B–C

23″ Early molded hair papier mache with unusual blue bow in back of hairdo. Has trunk, all hand made clothes, including hat box complete with hat. Trunk is marked: salesman's sample. Unjointed kid torso with wooden limbs. This type doll was made in Germany (primarily) from 1810. Courtesy Barbara Earnshaw.

V–W

15″ Clown with papier mache mask face and wire armiture body which makes the limbs moveable. All original with wire hoop. (Author).

B-C

REVALO

21" Bisque head with a long nose, blue glass eyes, painted lashes on bottom only, open mouth with four teeth, old mohair wig and on fully jointed composition body. Marks: REVALO/Germany/7½. Courtesy Irene Brown.

16" – D–E
21" – F–G

Bruno Schmidt character with protruding tongue. Sleep eyes and fully jointed composition body. Mold number 2097-6, along with heart. Courtesy Elizabeth Burke.

14" – E–F
18" – H–I
22" – I–J

15" Bisque head made by Bruno Schmidt and marked with a BSW, in a heart/Germany. Open mouth, mohair wig, set brown eyes and on a five piece bent leg baby body. Courtesy Gloyra Woods.

15" – E–F

SCHMIDT, BRUNO

22″ Called "Tommy Tucker" and marked with a BSW, in a heart. Made by Bruno Schmidt. Closed mouth, sleep eyes and molded hair. Body is composition. Courtesy Elaine Boyle.

16″ – M–N
22″ – O–Q

8½" Bisque head on five piece mache body. Pierced nostrils, human hair wig and dressed in old handmade clothes. Marks: F S & C 1295. Made by Franz Schmidt and Co. and very, very unusual in this size. Courtesy O.D. Gregg.

8½" D-E
15" – G-H
19" – I-J

SCHOENAU & HOFFMEISTNER
SIMON & HALBIG

24″ All original Princess Elizabeth. Bisque head with blue eyes and open mouth. Marks: Porzellan Fabric Burggrub Princess Elizabeth/6½/Made in Germany. Made by Schoenau & Hoffmeister. Courtesy Barbara Earnshaw.

18″ – Y–Z
24″ – Z–ZA

24″ German Lady doll with bisque swivel head on bisque shoulder plate, replaced cloth lady body, bisque lower arms, brown eyes and open mouth with four teeth. Auburn mohair Gibson Girl hairdo. Completely dressed with underskirt, Mary Widow corset, camisole, panties and two petticoats with one matching dress. Dress is of old fabric & of the style worn by Ella Maureen Buchanan dated 1898. The Buchanans were a well known family in St. Joseph, Mo. Doll is marked: S & H/1010 and made by Simon & Halbig. Courtesy Irene Brown.

24″ – H–I

21″ Fantastic Simon and Halbig mold number 1159 lady on marked lady Jumeau body and all original clothes that include garter belt with metal stays. Her extra items also include an ivory glove stretcher. Open mouth and fur lashes. The cape is attached to the top of the dress back. Courtesy Barbara Earnshaw.

21″ W-X

25½″ All original lady doll with composition body that has a small waist and molded bust. Head is marked: 1159 Germany/Simon & Halbig/S & H 10. The body is marked: Jumeau. Sleep brown eyes/lashes and open mouth. Courtesy Barbara Earnshaw.

25½″ – X–Y

19″ Bisque head with large blue eyes/lashes, closed mouth and modeled blonde hair. Cloth body with cryer, composition arms and legs. Head marked: Copr. by Grace C. Rockwell./Germany. This very rare doll was designed by Grace Corry Rockwell and head made by Simon and Halbig in Germany for her. Courtesy Barbara Earnshaw.

19″ – ZA–ZB

SIMON & HALBIG

Simon and Halbig mold number 1279 and unusual in that she has two teeth and cheek dimples. The body is composition and fully jointed. Courtesy Elizabeth Burke.

$$14'' \ - E-F$$
$$17'' \ - F-G$$
$$21'' \ - G-H$$

20" Bisque head marked: 1078/Germany Halbig/S & H/7½ on composition lady body. Blue sleep eyes, painted and real lashes, molded and feathered brows, pierced ears and open mouth with four teeth. Dressed in old taffeta skirt, tucked cotton blouse with leg-o-mutton sleeves. Courtesy Irene Brown.

16" – E–F
20" – F–G
25" – H–I

SIMON & HALBIG

15″ Head circumference baby with flirty eyes, tin eyelids, moveable tongue and on five piece bent leg baby body. Marks:
Ah   /Simon & Halbig/Made in Germany/156/12½.
W
Made for Adolf Hulss in 1915. Courtesy Irene Brown.

14″ – F–G
18″ – G–H
22″ – H–I

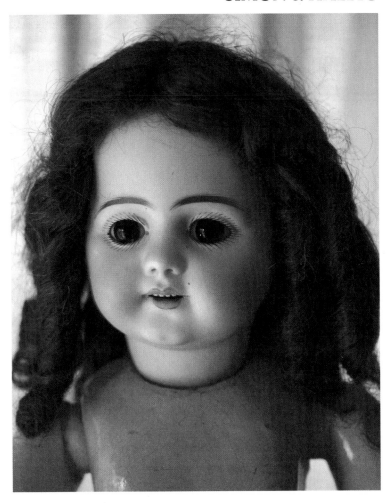

21″ Marks: S & H 719 DEP. Early Simon and Halbig bisque head made for Edison Phonograph tin body (replaced body). Large brown set eyes, heavy painted lashes around the eyes, red eye dots and in nostrils. Open mouth with six teeth. (There is also a closed mouth version of mold number 719). High forehead and deep cut in pate like French dolls. Mohair wig. Courtesy Irene Brown.

21″ – I-J

SIMON & HALBIG

22″ Bisque head with top of head uncut and three stringing holes. Blue set eyes, closed mouth. Marks: S 13 H 719 DEP. Courtesy Pat Landis.

22″ – O-P

Top of the head of the 719 mold number made by Simon and Halbig to show the cut out normally used (Line around mid-head) and how the head is actually cut and a plaster plug inserted. Courtesy Pat Landis.

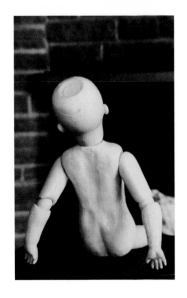

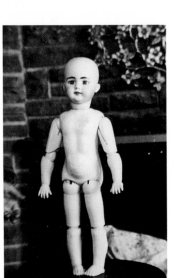

This is the body of the Simon and Halbig 719 character doll. The French scorned knee detail, where the German makers enjoyed detailing the knees. Courtesy Pat Landis.

18" Brown bisque head with fired in color, large set eyes and open mouth. On fully jointed brown composition body. Marks: S.H. 949. Courtesy Barbara Earnshaw.

18" – K–L

17" Head circumference is marked: 1489 Erika, hole cut in bisque, followed by /Simon & Halbig/14. Blue sleep eyes with lashes painted above and below. Pugged nose with molded nostrils and red dots. Open mouth with two lower teeth. Blonde mohair wig and on five piece bent leg baby body. Dressed in old Christening dress and tatted hat. Courtesy Irene Brown.

19" – T–U
25" – W–X

14" "New Born Baby" by Herm Steiner. Tiny, fine painted, upper and lower lashes, blue sleep eyes and celluloid marked with turtle hands. Cloth body and bisque head. Marks: 240/2/Made in Germany. Later ones were marked:240 or Herm Steiner. New Born Baby can be identified by the number 240 and the flat part on the tip of the nose. Steiner took Grace S. Putnam to court saying she copied his patent, but lost the case because his doll is only marked with a number and her's were signed. The Steiner doll was first on the market. It must be noted that Armand Marseille's doll "Baby Phyllis" also carries the 240 mold number. Courtesy Diane Hoffman.

14" – E–F

WOLF, LOUIS

15″ Head circumference marked: 48 L.W. & Co. 12. Molded and painted brush mark hair, light blue sleep eyes with painted lashes below and over. Open mouth with two teeth, tongue, and tiny cheek dimples and in chin. Dressed as a real baby with wool slip, fancy crochet trimmed slip, long dress, wool sacque and crocheted bonnet, plus long over the knee booties complete the outfit. Doll made for Louis Wolf and Company. Courtesy Irene Brown.

15″ – F–G
20″ – H–I

INDEX

123

REVISED PRICES FOR VOLUME I

Revised prices on dolls contained in Volume I of German Dolls, featuring character children & babies. The listing will be by page number.